Narcissistic Fathers: The Challenge of Being a Son or Daughter of a Narcissistic Father, and How to Overcome It. A Guide to Healing and Recovering After Covert

Alexandria Publications

Published by Digital Mind, 2024.

NARCISSISTIC FATHERS: THE CHALLENGE OF BEING A SON OR DAUGHTER OF A NARCISSISTIC FATHER, AND HOW TO OVERCOME IT. A GUIDE TO HEALING AND RECOVERING AFTER COVERT

First edition. January 24, 2024.

Copyright © 2024 Alexandria Publications.

ISBN: 979-8223388609

Written by Alexandria Publications.

Also by Alexandria Publications

Extreme Hypnosis for Rapid Weight Loss in Women: Learn How to Lose Weight with Hypnosis and Mental Power.
Learning to Manage Money: Financial Education from Childhood to Adolescence. Teaching Your Children to Save, Spend, and Invest Wisely
Narcissistic Fathers: The Challenge of Being a Son or Daughter of a Narcissistic Father, and How to Overcome It. A Guide to Healing and Recovering After Covert
Narcissistic Mothers: The Truth about Being a Daughter of a Narcissistic Mother, and How to Overcome It. A Guide to Healing and Recovering from Narcissistic Abuse.

Table of Contents

Introduction

Welcome to the journey of exploring one of the most complex and disturbing phenomena that can affect family dynamics : parental narcissism. This book dives into the depths of this delicate and often underappreciated topic, with the goal of shedding light on narcissistic behavior patterns that directly impact parenting and emotional development of children.

Into the very fabric of parenting , where unconditional love and support is expected to flourish, parental narcissism introduces a distorted dynamic. Narcissistic parents, with their insatiable desire for attention, lack of empathy, and emotional manipulation, weave a complex web that can leave deep scars on their children's self-esteem and psychological well-being.

Throughout these pages, we will explore not only the characteristics of parental narcissism, but also its concrete manifestations in everyday life. From excessive competition with one's own children to the inability to recognize their emotional needs, we will examine how these behavioral patterns affect the mental and emotional health of children, influencing their ability to forge healthy relationships in the future.

As we delve into this analysis, we will also provide practical tools for identifying and dealing with parental narcissism. From setting healthy boundaries to seeking emotional support and exploring therapeutic options, this book seeks to be a beacon of knowledge and guidance for those facing the unique challenge of having narcissistic parents.

Through stories of resilience, practical advice, and guidance from professionals in the field, we aim to offer not only a deeper understanding of this phenomenon, but also a path toward healing and building a full and conscious life.

Join us on this journey of understanding, healing, and empowerment as we unravel the complex threads of parental narcissism and explore the possibility of a healthier, more balanced future for those who have been impacted by this challenging reality.

Chapter 1: Definition and Characteristics of Narcissism

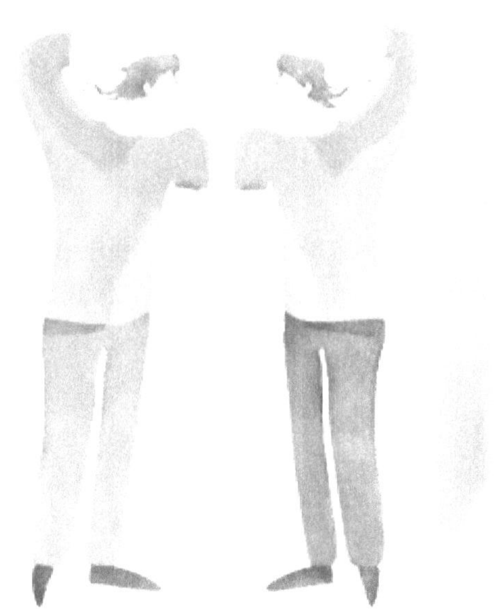

On the journey towards a deep understanding of the complex phenomenon of narcissism in adults, we delve into the very heart of its psychological foundations. This first chapter serves as a gateway to a thorough analysis of narcissism, exploring its roots in psychology, its dimensions, and the specific manifestations that manifest in adult dynamics.

1.1. Narcissism in Psychology

In the intricate universe of psychology, narcissism stands as a fascinating and often challenging phenomenon to understand. This psychological construct, rooted in Greek mythology with the myth of Narcissus, has found its way into the theories and practices of modern psychology, providing a lens through which we examine behavioral patterns and relational dynamics. Delving into the definition and characteristics of narcissism reveals a complex tapestry of self-perception, social interaction, and, in the context we explore here, the peculiar dynamics of narcissistic parenting .

Defining Narcissism: Beyond the Mythological Reflection . At its core, narcissism in psychology refers to a pattern of personality traits characterized by excessive self- focus , constant seeking of admiration, and a lack of empathy toward the needs and experiences of others. The root of the term comes from Narcissus, the young man in Greek mythology who fell in love with his own image reflected in a pond. While the mythological myth describes a literal fixation on image, psychological narcissism encompasses a broader range of behaviors and attitudes rooted in self-admiration .

Characteristics of Narcissism: A Look at the Internal Dynamics . The characteristics of narcissism, when manifested in personality, can create a distinctive set of observable behaviors. The constant search for admiration is one of the cornerstones, manifesting itself in an insatiable desire for attention and validation. Lack of empathy, another central component, results in an inability to connect emotionally with others, prioritizing one's own needs over those of others.

Fragile self-esteem, paradoxically covered by a façade of grandiosity, marks another characteristic trait. The underlying vulnerability leads to extreme susceptibility to criticism, which can result in defensive or even aggressive responses to protect the idealized self-image.

Dimensions of Narcissism: There is Not One, But Several Nuances . It is important to highlight that narcissism is not a homogeneous phenomenon; rather, it comes in several dimensions. Grandiose narcissism, on the one hand, is characterized by inflated self-evaluation and a belief in one's own superiority. On the other hand, vulnerable narcissism reveals a façade of grandiosity that hides fragile self-esteem and a deep sense of internal shame.

Narcissism in Parenting : The Challenge of Parenting from the Ego . When we transfer these characteristics to the area of parenting , a complex and often harmful scenario is unraveled. A narcissistic parent may perceive his children as extensions of himself, seeking to fulfill his own needs for validation through the achievements and successes of the offspring. Lack of empathy can translate into an inability to recognize and meet children's genuine emotional needs, creating an emotionally lacking environment.

The Challenge of Establishing Healthy Connections: Impact on the Parent -Child Relationship . The relationship between a narcissistic parent and their child can become an emotional battlefield. The child, eager for love and recognition, may find himself trapped in a cycle of constantly seeking parental approval. However, the narcissistic parent's lack of empathy and seeking admiration can create a painful dynamic of invalidation and dismissal of the child's legitimate emotional needs.

This challenge in forming healthy connections can have lasting consequences on a child's emotional development, affecting self-esteem, the ability to form meaningful relationships, and understanding of what it means to experience genuine, unconditional love.

The Psychology of Narcissism in Parenting : A Mirror for Reflection . By exploring narcissism in psychology and its manifestation in parenting , we delve into the complexities of self-image, relationships, and the lasting impact on family dynamics. This analysis does not seek to simplify or stigmatize, but rather to invite deep reflection on the dynamics that can affect the environment in which children grow and develop. Narcissism in parenting is a mirror that reflects challenges and complexities, and it is through understanding and awareness that we can begin to unravel its layers and seek paths to healing.

1.2. Manifestations of Narcissism in Parenting

Exploring narcissism in parenting involves delving into the concrete manifestations of this phenomenon in family dynamics. These manifestations, woven into the fabric of parenting, create an environment that deeply impacts the emotional development of children. Examining these manifestations closely reveals a complex landscape of behaviors that manifest in specific and often subtle ways.

1. **Conditional Validation: The Mirage of Unconditional Love** . One of the most prominent manifestations of narcissism in parenting is conditioned validation. Instead of offering unconditional love, the narcissistic parent tends to validate the child only based on his or her achievements or how those achievements reflect positively on the parent. This creates a mirage of acceptance, where love and validation

are transitory and dependent on the child's performance, generating a distorted sense of self-worth .

2. **Excessive Competition: The Race for Admiration** . The constant desire for admiration on the part of the narcissist can lead to excessive competition with one's own children. Instead of fostering an environment of mutual support and growth, the narcissistic parent sees their children as potential rivals. This competitive dynamic can manifest itself in constant comparisons, dismissal of the child's achievements, or even the appropriation of childhood successes to satisfy the insatiable need for self-recognition.

3. **Emotional Manipulation: The Subtle Technique of Control** . Emotional manipulation becomes a skillful tool in the hands of the narcissistic parent. With a masterful ability to read the child's needs and desires, the narcissist uses emotional manipulation to maintain subtle but firm control. This manipulation can manifest itself in various forms, from victimization to the strategic display of emotions to obtain what they want. Children, trapped in this game, may experience confusion and guilt, without fully understanding the forces acting on them.

4. **Dismissal of the Needs of the Child: A Silenced Echo** . The child's genuine emotional and psychological needs are often disregarded in the narcissistic environment. The narcissistic parent's lack of empathy prevents a real connection with the child's experiences and needs. The child may feel that their emotions are trivialized or ignored, creating an emotional void that impacts their perception of themselves and their abilities to establish meaningful relationships.

5. **Imposing Unrealistic Expectations: The Weight of Unattainable Expectations** . The narcissist, driven by his own quest for greatness, may impose unrealistic expectations on his children. The constant pressure to meet unattainable standards can result in an overwhelming burden for the child. This burden of unrealistic expectations can have significant consequences on the development of the child's self-concept , leading him to feel that he can never meet the exaggerated demands of the parent.

6. **Using Guilt as a Control Tool: Invisible Chains** . Narcissistic manipulation often uses blame as an effective tool of control. The child

may find himself chained by guilt, an emotion skillfully manipulated to maintain loyalty and submission. The narcissist, consciously or unconsciously, uses this tactic to ensure that the child remains in a role of caregiver or provider of the parent's emotional needs, thus perpetuating the narcissistic dynamic.

Chapter 2: Impact on Children

The bond between parents and children is essential for the emotional and psychological development of the latter. When this bond is affected by parental narcissism, the consequences can be significant and long-lasting. In this second chapter, we will closely explore how parents' narcissism impacts their children, leaving emotional traces that last over time.

2.1 Emotional and Psychological Effects of the Impact on Children

Let's delve into the intricate fabric of how the dynamic of narcissistic parents leaves a deep mark on the emotional and psychological world of their children. When parents are shrouded in the veil of narcissism, the emotional effects on their children can be significant. One of the most notable impacts is the development of self-esteem. Children who grow up in the shadow of narcissistic parents often face challenges in building a positive self-image. Parents' constant search for validation can leave children feeling inadequate and questioning their own worth.

The relationship between the child and the narcissistic parent can also affect the former's ability to form healthy relationships in the future. The chronic need for attention and constant competition can sow seeds of insecurity, making it difficult for children to trust others and form meaningful connections.

The mantle of parental narcissism often shapes children's perception of themselves. The constant seeking of approval from a narcissistic parent can lead to the internalization of negative self-talk. Children can adopt relentless self-criticism, constantly seeking perfection to obtain that flash of approval that rarely comes.

On a psychological level, children of narcissistic parents may face challenges in developing coping skills. Lack of emotional support and focus on the father's needs can leave children feeling alone in the midst of difficulties. This can result in a limited ability to handle stress and life's adversities.

Emotional manipulation, a common tactic in interacting with narcissistic parents, also leaves its mark. Children may develop extreme sensitivity to the emotional signals of others as a result of having been constantly alert to their parents' changing needs. This can lead to emotional hypervigilance and constant concern for the well-being of others, sometimes to the detriment of your own needs.

The lack of clear boundaries in the dynamic with a narcissistic parent can also have negative consequences. Children may experience difficulty setting healthy boundaries in their relationships and may find themselves trapped in patterns of codependency, constantly seeking external approval and validation.

These emotional and psychological effects are just glimpses of the complexity that surrounds parenting under the shadow of parental narcissism. Children, shaped by these dynamics, carry with them the invisible scars that affect their emotional well-being and the way they relate to themselves and the world around them.

2.2 Development of Self-Esteem in Children of Narcissistic Parents

This journey leads us to understand how interaction with a parent with narcissistic traits can shape the perception that children have of themselves, marking a complex path towards the construction of a healthy self-image.

In the area of self-esteem, children of narcissistic parents often face significant challenges. The constant need for validation from parents can sow the seeds of doubt and insecurity in a child's heart. Self-esteem, that essential foundation for self-confidence, can be undermined when attention and praise are conditional and elusive.

Selective praise is a common parenting tool in homes with a narcissistic parent. Children may find that their parents' approval is closely linked to external achievements and the ability to meet unrealistic expectations. This conditional approach can generate a fragile self-esteem dependent on external approval.

The lack of genuine recognition of individual achievements also impacts children's self-evaluation. When successes are overshadowed by parents' needs, children may internalize the belief that they are never good enough. This pattern of thinking can persist into adult life, affecting the way they face challenges and seek validation in various areas.

Constant competition with narcissistic parents for attention and approval can lead to constant comparison with others. Children may internalize the belief that their worth is directly related to their ability to stand out from the crowd. This comparative approach can lead to distorted self-evaluation, where self-worth is measured in terms of superiority over others.

The cycle of seeking approval and validation can become a constant in these children's lives. Self-esteem can be intricately linked to external response, creating a vulnerability to criticism and an insatiable need for recognition. The inability to find security in one's own worth, regardless of external approval, becomes emotionally burdensome.

The impact on the development of self-esteem is a sensitive and crucial aspect when exploring how children of narcissistic parents navigate the complex emotional world. This analysis leads us to reflect on the importance of fostering an environment where self-esteem can flourish in a healthy way, far from the shadows of parental narcissism.

Chapter 3: Patterns of Narcissistic Behavior in Parenting

In the journey of understanding the impact of narcissistic parents on their children, it is crucial to closely examine the specific behavioral patterns that characterize this form of parenting. This third chapter delves into the daily dynamics that define the relationship between narcissistic parents and children, exploring how these behaviors influence the emotional and psychological development of the little ones.

3.1. Emotional Manipulation in Narcissistic Parenting

Here we encounter a deeply rooted and potentially harmful aspect: emotional manipulation and how it is woven into the daily interactions between narcissistic parents and their children.

Emotional manipulation, in the context of narcissistic parenting , manifests itself in diverse but powerful ways. One of the key elements is the use of children's emotions as a tool to maintain control. Narcissistic parents, in their constant search for validation and attention, may resort to subtle tactics to influence their children's emotions, creating unstable emotional ground.

A common method of emotional manipulation is blaming . Narcissistic parents, skilled masters of the art of deflecting responsibility, can make their children feel guilty for expressing needs or desires that compete with the parent's demands. This tactic creates an environment where children can doubt the legitimacy of their own emotions, perpetuating a cycle of subtle but effective manipulation.

Victimization is another frequently used strategy. Narcissistic parents may portray themselves as victims, making their children feel the burden of meeting their emotional needs. This victim role not only diverts attention from parental responsibilities, but also manipulates children's emotions by generating a sense of obligation and guilt.

Emotional invalidation is an additional component of manipulation in narcissistic parenting . Parents may minimize or ignore their children's legitimate emotions, dismissing their feelings and experiences. This invalidation creates an environment where children may begin to question the validity of their own emotions, contributing to emotional confusion and constant seeking of approval.

Emotional manipulation can also manifest itself through the fluctuation between overvaluation and devaluation. Narcissistic parents can alternate between excessive praise and relentless criticism, creating a volatile emotional state in their children. This pattern can leave children constantly seeking validation, never sure where they stand on the scale of parental approval.

Emotional manipulation in narcissistic parenting leaves invisible scars in the emotional world of the children. Emotional confusion, self-doubt, and the constant need to satisfy parents' emotional demands are some of the consequences that can last into adulthood. By exploring this aspect, we shed light on how emotional manipulation can become an intrinsic component of narcissistic parenting and its lasting effects on the emotional well-being of children.

3.2. Lack of Empathy in Narcissistic Parenting

Within the complex plot of narcissistic behavior patterns in parenting, there is a central and revealing element: the lack of empathy. This lack affects the daily interactions between narcissistic parents and their children, leaving a deep mark on the very fabric of the parental relationship.

The lack of empathy in narcissistic parenting manifests itself in the parents' inability to connect emotionally with their children's experiences and needs. Instead of responding sensitively to their children's emotions, narcissistic parents may focus disproportionately on their own needs and desires, creating an emotional imbalance in the family dynamic.

One of the most obvious aspects of this lack of empathy is the difficulty in recognizing and responding to children's emotional signals. Narcissistic parents, wrapped up in their own concerns and desires, may overlook the legitimate emotional needs of their children. This lack of recognition can leave children feeling misunderstood and alone in their emotional struggles.

Lack of emotional validation is another consequence of lack of empathy in narcissistic parenting. Children may experience difficulties expressing their emotions openly, fearing a lack of response or minimization of their feelings by their parents. This dynamic can lead to emotional disconnection, where children learn to repress their emotional needs to avoid rejection.

The lack of empathy is also reflected in the inability of narcissistic parents to put themselves in their children's shoes. Parenting decisions and actions may be driven primarily by the narcissistic needs of the parent, without fully considering the impact on the emotional well-being of the children. This lack of consideration can breed resentment and contribute to the perception of children as simple extensions of their parents.

In the realm of narcissistic parenting, a lack of empathy can lead to a dynamic of constant invalidation. Parents can minimize their children's experiences and feelings, creating an environment where emotional expression is constantly underestimated. This repeated invalidation can have significant consequences on the emotional development of children, affecting their ability to establish healthy relationships in adult life.

The lack of empathy in narcissistic parenting leads us to understand how emotional disconnection directly impacts the emotional world of children. The constant search for validation and recognition collides with the lack of empathic response, creating a complex emotional dance that leaves children navigating turbulent waters on their journey toward self-affirmation and emotional understanding.

3.3. Competition with Children in Narcissistic Parenting

Competition with children, in the context of narcissistic parenting , manifests itself in several ways. A fundamental aspect is the constant search to highlight the achievements and abilities of one's own children. Narcissistic parents, driven by the need for external validation, may feel the urge to demonstrate their superiority, sometimes overshadowing their children's legitimate achievements.

This competition can influence the goals and aspirations of children. The constant pressure to meet unrealistic expectations from narcissistic parents can lead children to develop a distorted perception of what constitutes success. Self-evaluation can be intricately linked to the ability to excel in comparison to parents, creating a cycle of constant competition.

The lack of genuine recognition of children's individual achievements is another aspect of this competition. Although narcissistic parents may superficially praise their children's successes, this approval is often conditional on constant validation of parental superiority. Individual achievements may go unnoticed or minimized, contributing to a feeling of inadequacy in children.

The impact on self-esteem is a crucial component of competence with children. Children may internalize the belief that their worth is directly tied to their ability to meet parental expectations. This close connection between performance and self-worth can create a significant emotional burden, leaving children in a constant search for approval.

Competition can also lead to tense family dynamics. The need to stand out can become a source of conflict, as children may feel constant pressure to meet unrealistic expectations. This dynamic can affect family cohesion, creating an environment where parental validation becomes an emotional currency.

The constant struggle for approval and validation can shape children's emotional development, leaving invisible scars that last into adulthood. That is to say, subtle but powerful competition between parents and children can influence children's self-esteem and perception of personal worth.

Chapter 4: Cycle of Narcissistic Abuse in the Family

Living in a home with narcissistic parents can be like navigating turbulent waters. This chapter delves into the cycle of narcissistic abuse that often characterizes family dynamics affected by parental narcissism. We will explore how this cycle unfolds, from the initial phases to the control strategies that perpetuate the dysfunctional dynamic.

4.1. Phases of the Narcissistic Abuse Cycle in the Family

<u>**First phase: Idealization and Enchantment**</u>

The cycle of narcissistic abuse begins with the idealization phase, where the narcissist displays charms to gain the trust and devotion of the family. At this stage, children may experience apparent overvaluation, receiving excessive attention and excessive praise. This charm creates an illusion of harmony and affection, establishing the basis for unconditional acceptance by the family.

Second phase: Disenchantment and Criticism

As the family adapts to the initial charm, the phase of disenchantment emerges. Here, the narcissist reveals his inability to maintain constant idealization. Criticism is introduced subtly, eroding the children's self-esteem. Attention and praise that once flowed generously can turn into derogatory comments and put-downs, sowing the seeds of self-deception and confusion in the family.

Third phase: Devaluation and Manipulation

The devaluation deepens in the third phase, where the narcissist intensifies emotional manipulation. Children may find themselves on volatile emotional terrain, desperately seeking the approval that now seems to elude them. Subtle manipulation, often wrapped in a cloak of victimization, creates an environment where the family feels obligated to satisfy narcissistic needs, even if this means sacrificing their own needs and well-being.

Fourth phase: Withdrawal and Punishment

In the withdrawal phase, the narcissist withdraws emotionally, punishing the family with his emotional absence. Attention and validation, once easily accessible, become scarce. Children may face prolonged silences, creating anxiety and confusion. This withdrawal is often an act of control, where the narcissist seeks to assert their power by keeping the family in a state of constant anticipation.

Fifth phase: Temporary Reconciliation and Renewed Cycle

The final phase of the narcissistic abuse cycle is temporary reconciliation. The narcissist may once again deploy charm and praise, seeking to reestablish emotional connection. Children, longing for approval and stability, can fall back into the trap of idealization. However, this reconciliation is short-lived, as it soon fades away to give way to a new round of the cycle.

This analysis of the phases of the narcissistic abuse cycle highlights the repetitive and manipulative nature of this pattern. The family becomes trapped in an emotional dance, constantly seeking approval and affection that the narcissist strategically grants and withdraws. Understanding these phases is essential to unraveling the complexity of family dynamics under the shadow of narcissistic abuse.

4.2. Control Strategies

a. **Constant Emotional Manipulation** . A central strategy in the narcissist's arsenal is constant emotional manipulation. Uses tactics such as invalidating the emotions of others, minimizing the legitimate experiences of family members. This manipulation creates an environment where children can doubt the validity of their own feelings, falling into the trap of emotional confusion.

b. **Victimization and Blame** . Victimization is another sharp tool in the narcissistic control strategy. The narcissist may portray himself as the victim, creating feelings of guilt in the family. This tactic not only diverts attention from the narcissist's actions, but also manipulates the children's emotions by making them feel responsible for the parent's needs and desires.

c. **Distortion of Reality** . Reality distortion is a subtle but powerful tactic that the narcissist uses to maintain control. You can reinterpret past events, change the narrative, and deny obvious facts. This manipulation of reality leaves the family questioning their own perception of events, creating fertile ground for mind control.

d. **Silence and Emotional Withdrawal** . Silence and emotional withdrawal are strategies that reinforce the family's emotional dependence on the narcissist. By withdrawing, the narcissist punishes the family with his emotional absence, generating anxiety and fear. This tactic reinforces the idea that the narcissist's affection and approval are scarce resources that must be earned through submission.

e. **Conditional Praise and Constant Competition** . Conditional praise and constant competition are strategies designed to keep the family in a constant state of seeking validation. Although the narcissist may give superficial praise, this praise is closely tied to constant validation of parental superiority . Constant competition creates a dynamic of comparison that reinforces the family's dependence on narcissistic recognition.

f. **Financial and Material Control** . Financial and material control is another facet of control strategies. The narcissist may use financial position to keep the family tied to his needs and desires. This material control creates financial dependency, making it difficult for the family to set boundaries or question the narcissist's actions.

These control strategies are fundamental gears in the mechanism of the cycle of narcissistic abuse in the family. They work together to keep family members in a constant state of emotional dependence and approval-seeking. Understanding these tactics is essential to dismantling the narcissistic control network and beginning the healing process within the family.

Chapter 5: Identification and Diagnosis

In this chapter, we delve into the task of recognizing narcissistic patterns, understanding their distinctive signs, and exploring the tools that psychology offers us to accurately diagnose this complex construct.

5.1. Signs of a Narcissistic Parent: Identification and Diagnosis

Excessive Need for Validation and Admiration . A hallmark sign of a narcissistic parent is an excessive need for validation and admiration. This parent constantly seeks the approval of others, seeking to have their self-esteem reinforced through praise and recognition. This insatiable need can lead to a dynamic where children feel constant pressure to meet the unrealistic expectations of the narcissistic parent.

Lack of Empathy and Consideration towards the Needs of Children . Lack of empathy is a key characteristic that manifests in the narcissistic parent's inability to understand and respond to their children's emotional needs. Instead of connecting emotionally, this parent may focus disproportionately on his or her own needs, leaving the children feeling misunderstood and neglected.

Constant Competition with Children . Constant competition with children is another telltale sign. The narcissistic parent may feel the need to highlight the achievements and abilities of their own children, creating a dynamic where parental validation is linked to the parent's superiority. This competition can generate pressure and anxiety in children, affecting their self-esteem and perception of personal worth.

Emotional Manipulation and Victimization . Emotional manipulation and victimization are strategies that the narcissistic parent uses to maintain control. They may portray themselves as victims, generating feelings of guilt in the family. This subtle manipulation diverts attention from the narcissistic parent's actions, creating an environment where the children feel an obligation to meet the parent's emotional needs.

Conditional Praise and Constant Devaluation . Conditional praise and constant devaluation are patterns that may indicate the presence of a narcissistic parent. Although they may give superficial praise, this praise is often conditional on constant validation of parental superiority. Devaluation, on the other hand, can manifest itself through constant criticism and disqualification, eroding the children's self-esteem.

Inability to Recognize Errors and Responsibilities . The inability to recognize mistakes and take responsibility is a key sign. The narcissistic parent may have difficulty admitting faults, preferring to deflect responsibility or reinterpret events. This lack of accountability can create an environment where children learn to doubt their own perceptions and experiences.

Cycles of Idealization and Disenchantment in Family Relationships . Cycles of idealization and disenchantment in family relationships are repetitive patterns that indicate the presence of a narcissistic parent. This parent may display initial charms to win the family's devotion, but these periods of idealization are followed by phases of disenchantment, where criticism and devaluation come into play.

Recognizing these signs is essential to understanding the dynamics of narcissistic parenting. Early identification can open doors to coping and support strategies, providing valuable tools to address challenges that arise in the context of narcissistic parenting.

5.2. Professional Evaluation in the Identification and Diagnosis of Narcissistic Parents

In the fifth chapter of our journey toward understanding narcissistic parents, we delve into the crucial terrain of professional evaluation. This process plays a vital role in identifying and diagnosing narcissistic parenting patterns. Through different tools and approaches, professionals, such as psychologists and therapists, seek to decipher the complexities of family dynamics and offer strategies adapted to each situation.

<u>Clinical Interviews: The Voice of Experience</u>

Clinical interviews are shining beacons that illuminate the assessment journey. In these interactions, professionals not only listen to parents' narratives, but observe their behavior, facial expressions, and tone of voice. These interviews offer a window into family dynamics, allowing professionals to discern patterns of narcissistic behavior, such as excessive need for validation or lack of empathy.

<u>Behavioral Observation: A Family X-ray</u>

Observing behavior in everyday family situations is like getting an x-ray of daily life. Professionals examine how the narcissistic parent relates to the children, how they handle stressful situations, and how they respond to the family's emotional needs. This hands-on approach provides valuable insight into relational dynamics, identifying potential signs of narcissism that may not be evident in a clinical setting.

<u>Analysis of Empathy and Recognition of Children's Needs</u>

A parent's ability to express empathy and recognize their children's emotional needs is a crucial indicator. During assessment, professionals look for signs of a lack of empathy, such as an inability to understand children's experiences. This in-depth analysis reveals whether the parent can adequately respond to the emotional needs of the children or whether these are overshadowed by the parent's own demands.

Exploring Family History: Weaving the Tapestry of Narcissism

Family history is a treasure trove of information that helps weave the tapestry of narcissism. Practitioners explore patterns over time, looking for repetitive cycles of idealization and disenchantment, as well as the presence of emotional manipulation. Understanding how the parent's past relationships influence current dynamics provides a more complete view of narcissistic tendencies in parenting.

Assessment of Parenting Skills and Stress Responses

The parenting skills assessment is like a mirror that reflects the parent's ability to adapt to the changing needs of the children. Professionals observe how the parent handles challenging situations and whether they show flexibility in their approaches. Disproportionate responses to stress or rigidity in parenting practices may be indicators of narcissistic traits.

Error Recognition and Learning: The Key to Adaptability

The parent's willingness to acknowledge mistakes and learn from experiences is an important key. Professionals explore whether the parent can take responsibility and address areas for improvement. Reluctance to acknowledge mistakes or deflect responsibility may be a sign of narcissistic traits that impact the parent's ability to adapt and learn.

Analysis of the Therapeutic Relationship: A Mirror of Potential Change

The therapeutic relationship is like a mirror that reflects the potential for change. Professionals assess the parent's willingness to participate in the therapeutic process, their ability to establish a genuine connection, and their openness to change. Resistance to introspection or lack of commitment may influence the overall assessment of the presence of narcissistic traits.

This professional assessment, using a range of tools and approaches, allows for a deeper understanding of the presence of narcissistic traits in parenting. It is an essential step in designing effective intervention strategies and providing the support necessary to promote healthier family dynamics.

Chapter 6: Facing the Challenge: Strategies for Coping with a Narcissistic Parent

In the sixth chapter, we dive into the challenging task of confronting a narcissistic parent. The "Establishing Healthy Boundaries" subsection becomes a practical compass for those seeking to balance authenticity and self-protection in the context of a complex relationship with a narcissistic parent.

6.1. Establishing Healthy Boundaries: Navigating the Terrain with a Narcissistic Parent

Recognizing the Importance of Personal Boundaries

Setting healthy boundaries begins with fundamentally recognizing the importance of personal boundaries. It is imperative to understand that setting boundaries is not an act of selfishness, but rather an essential need to preserve emotional health and maintain equitable relationships. Accepting that it is valid to have individual needs and limits is the foundation on which the ability to deal with a narcissistic parent effectively is built.

Clarity in Communication: Direct and Assertive

Clear communication becomes a powerful tool when setting boundaries with a narcissistic parent. Opting for direct and assertive clarity is essential. Expressing simply and firmly what personal boundaries are and what behaviors are unacceptable establishes a clear framework for interaction. Avoiding ambiguity and vagueness is key to preventing misunderstandings and manipulations by the narcissistic parent.

Defining Clear and Coherent Consequences

Setting effective limits involves defining clear and consistent consequences if those limits are violated. Establishing the repercussions of certain narcissistic behaviors in advance provides a solid structure. This foresight reduces potential manipulation by the narcissistic parent by making it clear that actions have predictable consequences.

Learning to Say "No" Without Guilt

The ability to say "no" without feeling overwhelmed by guilt is an art that is honed when facing a narcissistic parent. Recognizing that saying "no" is not an act of disloyalty, but rather a healthy assertion of boundaries, is essential. Freeing yourself from the emotional burden associated with rejecting narcissistic demands allows you to establish firm boundaries without sacrificing your own integrity.

Prioritizing Your Own Emotional Well-being

Setting healthy boundaries means prioritizing your own emotional well-being. This act not only protects against narcissistic manipulation, but also sets a precedent for self-worth and self-care. Recognizing that self-care is not selfish, but essential, is the cornerstone of building a more balanced relationship with a narcissistic parent.

Maintaining Emotional Distance when Necessary

Emotional distance becomes a crucial tactic when confronting a narcissistic parent. Learning to maintain a healthy emotional connection while setting boundaries can involve moments of distancing when necessary. This measure does not imply a total rejection, but rather a step to preserve one's mental health in situations that may be emotionally exhausting.

Seeking External Support and Resources

Setting healthy boundaries is strengthened by seeking external support and accessing available resources. Connecting with friends, family, or others who have faced similar challenges provides a valuable support network. Exploring resources such as books, online support groups, or individual therapy can offer additional insights and effective strategies.

Setting healthy boundaries when confronting a narcissistic parent is a dynamic process that involves a careful balance between personal authenticity and emotional protection. Recognizing the importance of boundaries, communicating clearly, defining consequences, learning to say "no" without guilt, prioritizing one's own well-being, maintaining emotional distance when necessary, and seeking external support become powerful tools for those seeking to confront this. challenge with resilience and self-care.

6.2. Seeking Emotional Support: An Anchor in the Journey of Coping with a Narcissistic Parent

"Seeking Emotional Support" becomes an essential anchor in the emotional journey, providing the sustenance necessary to navigate the complexities of this unique relationship.

Sharing Experiences with Trusted People . Opening your heart and sharing experiences with trusted people stands as the first pillar of seeking emotional support. Whether close friends, family, or trusted colleagues, having a space to express the emotions and challenges associated with a narcissistic parent eases the emotional burden. The empathy and understanding of these confidants can be a valuable source of support.

Exploring Support Groups and Online Communities . Connecting with support groups and online communities is presented as an accessible and enriching option. The uniqueness of the experience in facing a narcissistic parent is shared with those who have gone through similar challenges. These spaces offer fertile ground for exchanging practical advice, effective strategies, and most importantly, the emotional validation that is often missing in relationships with narcissistic parents.

Seeking Professional Advice . Seeking professional advice stands as a cornerstone in building a robust emotional support system. Psychologists, therapists, and counselors have the tools and experience necessary to guide those facing a narcissistic parent. These professionals not only offer unbiased perspectives, but also facilitate specific strategies for dealing with the emotional challenges that arise from this relationship.

Establishing Boundaries with the Support of Professionals . Emotional support also translates into the ability to set boundaries with the support of professionals. Therapists can offer specific guidance on how to effectively communicate boundaries and manage the narcissistic parent's potential reactions. This collaboration with professionals creates a space where the individual can build personalized and sustainable strategies to protect their emotional well-being.

Participating in Self-Care Activities . Seeking emotional support is not only limited to interacting with other people, but also encompasses engaging in self-care activities. These activities act as a balm for the soul, providing moments of relief and renewal. From the practice of meditation to immersion in passionate hobbies, these experiences become a fundamental anchor in the midst of emotional storms.

Creating Spaces for Self-Compassion and Internal Validation . Self-compassion and internal validation emerge as intrinsic sources of emotional support. Recognizing and accepting one's emotions, without judgment, becomes an act of self-love. Cultivating an internal narrative that reflects the reality of the situation and the constant effort to confront it strengthens emotional resilience.

Establishing Clear Boundaries for Your Own Mental Health . Seeking emotional support ultimately involves establishing clear boundaries for one's own mental health. Recognizing when it is necessary to distance yourself, seek help or simply rest becomes a crucial skill. These boundaries not only protect emotional well-being, but also offer a constant reminder of the importance of putting mental health at the forefront.

Seeking emotional support when facing a narcissistic parent stands as an act of authenticity and strength. Through meaningful connections with others, professional counseling, engaging in self-care activities, and cultivating a compassionate relationship with yourself, a strong emotional scaffolding is built. This support becomes the compass that guides those facing the challenge of a narcissistic parent toward authenticity, self-care, and emotional resilience .

6.3. Therapy and Counseling: The Lighthouse in the Journey of Coping with a Narcissistic Parent

"Therapy and Counseling" become the beacon that guides the emotional journey, offering a structured path for those seeking to understand, heal and build practical strategies.

Exploring the Healing Power of Individual Therapy

Individual therapy emerges as a sacred space to explore the emotional impact of having a narcissistic parent. A trained therapist acts as a guide, providing a safe ground to express emotions, unravel thought patterns, and develop strategies to cope with challenges. Individual therapy is a personalized beacon that illuminates areas of growth and transformation.

Family Therapy: Navigating Relational Dynamics

Family therapy stands as a beacon that illuminates relational dynamics. In this space, family members, including the narcissistic parent, can work together to understand and address dysfunctional patterns. Family therapy offers a neutral ground where you can establish healthy boundaries and explore new forms of communication that foster more equitable relationships.

Couples Therapy: Addressing Relational Challenges

When the relationship with the narcissistic parent affects the couple's dynamic, couples therapy becomes a beacon that illuminates the tumultuous waters. Here, couples can address how parental dynamics influence their relationship, develop mutual support strategies, and strengthen emotional connection. Couples therapy acts as a roadmap to building a strong bond amidst external challenges.

Group Therapy: Sharing Experiences and Strategies

Group therapy presents itself as a collective beacon, where individuals who share similar challenges can find solace and valuable perspectives. This space provides a platform to share experiences, learn effective strategies, and receive support from those who understand the complexity of having a narcissistic parent. Group therapy becomes a guiding light through the healing power of community.

Psychological Counseling: Developing Personalized Strategies

Psychological counseling is positioned as a lighthouse that guides the development of personalized strategies. Counselors offer specialized guidance to address specific challenges, such as setting boundaries, managing narcissistic manipulation, and cultivating emotional resilience. This type of advice becomes a precise compass that directs efforts towards practical and sustainable solutions.

Cognitive-Behavioral Therapy: Transforming Thought Patterns

Cognitive-behavioral therapy stands as a beacon that illuminates the transformation of thought patterns. This therapeutic approach helps identify and change dysfunctional thoughts, promoting a more balanced and adaptive perspective. Cognitive behavioral therapy acts as a flashlight that reveals the tools to overcome deep-rooted emotional challenges.

Solution Focused Therapy: Focusing on Personal Growth

Solution-focused therapy becomes a beacon that focuses attention on personal growth. This therapeutic approach focuses on identifying and amplifying individual strengths, promoting the development of strategies that foster resilience and emotional well-being. Solution-focused therapy acts as a guiding light that directs you toward the path of growth and self-reflection.

Through these resources, you will find the guidance needed to understand, heal, and develop strategies that promote an emotionally balanced life. Each therapeutic and counseling approach becomes a light that highlights different aspects of the path, providing support and direction in the search for authenticity and emotional well-being.

Chapter 7: Healing from Wounds: Recovering from Parental Narcissism

Here we enter into sensitive terrain: the identification and diagnosis of this psychological phenomenon. This chapter serves as a beacon of knowledge for those seeking to understand the hallmark signs of narcissism, unravel its complexities, and ultimately explore the tools that psychology provides to accurately diagnose this multifaceted construct.

7.1. Healing Process: Navigating the Waters of Recovery

The "Healing Process" is extremely important in tumultuous emotional wounds, as it offers a route to heal and move towards a fuller life.

Step number one: Recognizing and Validating Emotions .

The first step in the healing process involves acknowledging and validating emotions. Allowing yourself to feel and express pain, confusion and frustration is essential. This act of authenticity lays the foundation for healing by making space for emotional truth, releasing the weight of past experiences.

Step Number Two: Establishing Healthy Boundaries in Relationships

During the healing process, there is a need to establish healthy boundaries in relationships. Learning to say "no" when necessary and clearly defining what is acceptable and unacceptable in personal interactions becomes a crucial tool. These boundaries act as protective guardians of emotional health, preserving the space necessary for recovery.

Step number three: Practicing Self-Acceptance and Self-Love

Self -acceptance and self-love emerge as beacons that illuminate the path to healing. Recognizing and embracing one's own worth, regardless of narcissistic parental expectations, becomes an essential practice. Building a positive relationship with yourself acts as a balm that soothes emotional wounds, fostering resilience and personal empowerment.

Step number four: Cultivating Relationships of Support and Companionship

Healing is strengthened by cultivating relationships of support and companionship. Connecting with friends, family, or support groups who understand the complexities of parental narcissism creates an environment in which mutual understanding and support flourish. These relationships act as community beacons, offering comfort and encouragement in the journey of recovery.

Step number five: Seeking the Necessary Professional Advice .

The healing process benefits greatly from seeking the necessary professional advice. Trained psychologists, therapists and counselors guide the process, offering tools and strategies tailored to individual needs. This professional collaboration becomes a specialized beacon that illuminates specific areas of the healing journey.

Step number six: Practicing Self-Care Regularly

The regular practice of self-care is presented as a beacon that highlights the importance of maintaining emotional well-being. From relaxing activities to healthy routines, self-care becomes a ritual that nourishes and strengthens.

This constant practice reinforces emotional resilience and acts as a guiding light towards emotional stability.

Step Number Seven: Developing a Sense of Purpose and Authenticity

Healing is completed by developing a sense of purpose and authenticity. Exploring personal passions, goals, and values creates a solid framework for building a meaningful and authentic life. This inner lighthouse directs towards self-realization and the construction of a life narrative that goes beyond the limitations imposed by parental narcissism.

The healing process, as a journey of emotional navigation, involves recognizing and validating emotions, setting healthy boundaries, practicing self-acceptance , cultivating supportive relationships, seeking professional counseling, practicing self-care, and developing a sense of purpose. Each of these elements become beacons that illuminate different aspects of the recovery path, offering direction and hope to those seeking to heal from the wounds of parental narcissism.

7.2. Building Healthy Relationships: Rebuilding Bonds After Parental Narcissism

Building Healthy Relationships becomes a practical guide that illuminates the path to more equitable and enriching relationships, marking a crucial stage in the recovery process.

Unlearning Harmful Relational Patterns

The process of building healthy relationships begins with unlearning unhealthy relational patterns acquired during interaction with a narcissistic parent. Identifying and reflecting on toxic behaviors allows us to open space for the adoption of new forms of communication and emotional connection. This step is essential to building relationships based on mutual respect and equity.

Fostering Open and Authentic Communication

The foundation of healthy relationships is founded on open and authentic communication. Practicing the honest expression of thoughts and feelings, as well as fostering a space where others can also share freely, creates fertile ground for mutual understanding. Communication becomes the bridge that unites people in a genuine and enriching dialogue.

Establishing Clear and Respectful Boundaries

Building healthy relationships involves setting clear and respectful boundaries. The ability to effectively communicate what is acceptable and what is not in a relationship contributes to an environment in which both parties feel valued and understood. These boundaries act as guardians of relational health, preserving harmony and balance.

Practicing Empathy and Mutual Understanding

The practice of empathy and mutual understanding becomes a beacon that illuminates the path to healthy relationships. Taking the time to understand the perspectives and experiences of others, as well as being understood in turn, strengthens emotional bonds. Empathy acts as a bridge that connects people on a deeper level.

Cultivating Trust Through Consistency

Building healthy relationships involves cultivating trust through consistency. Keeping promises, being reliable, and showing authenticity all contribute to building an environment of trust. Consistency becomes the foundation on which a solid and lasting connection is built.

Valuing and Respecting Individual Differences

In the process of building healthy relationships, valuing and respecting individual differences stands out as an essential practice. Recognizing that each person is unique, with their own perspectives and experiences, fosters acceptance and diversity in the relationship. This recognition contributes to an environment in which each individual feels seen and appreciated.

Nurturing Reciprocal and Equitable Relationships

Building healthy relationships involves nurturing reciprocal and equitable bonds. Reciprocity becomes the driving force that maintains balance in the relationship, where both parties contribute significantly to mutual growth and well-being. This equitable approach creates fertile ground for lasting and enriching relationships.

Learning and Growing Together

Building healthy relationships is a continuous journey of learning and growing together. Recognizing that people evolve and that relationships also go through changes allows us to adapt and adjust to changing needs. This dynamic approach contributes to the sustainability and vitality of the emotional connection.

Building healthy relationships after facing parental narcissism becomes a journey of reinvention and discovery. Unlearning unhealthy patterns, encouraging open communication, setting respectful boundaries, practicing empathy, cultivating trust, valuing individual differences, nurturing equitable relationships, and learning and growing together are essential steps to building bonds that nourish the soul and foster authenticity in life. path of recovery.

Chapter 8: Legal Intervention and Child Protection

This is a critical and socially relevant area: legal intervention and child protection. This chapter not only highlights the pressing need to address the legal ramifications of parental narcissism, but also stands as a beacon of awareness and action to protect the well-being of children who may be affected by narcissistic dynamics in the family environment.

8.1. Custody and Visitation in Cases of Parental Narcissism

a. **Assessment of Family Dynamics by Competent Professionals** . If parental narcissism is suspected, it is essential to begin with a thorough evaluation of family dynamics by competent professionals. Psychologists, social workers and other mental health experts can offer specialized insight into understanding the impact of narcissistic behavior on the family environment. This evaluation acts as the first stage to inform any legal intervention.

b. **Development of Detailed Documentation of Incidents and Behavior Patterns** . Building a strong legal case requires detailed documentation of incidents and behavioral patterns related to parental narcissism. Keeping records of inappropriate interactions, communications, and behavior provides tangible evidence to support any legal request. Meticulous documentation becomes the pillar on which legal intervention is built.

c. **Lawyers Specialized in Family Law: Key Allies** . Facing cases of parental narcissism demands the advice of lawyers specialized in family law. These professionals become key allies, providing specific legal guidance and developing strategies to address the complexities of the case. Choosing an attorney with experience in parental narcissism cases is crucial to ensuring effective representation.

d. **Presentation of Substantial Evidence in Legal Hearings** . The presentation of substantial evidence in legal hearings stands as an essential task. Detailed documentation and legal advice converge at this point, supporting the presentation of concrete evidence demonstrating the impact of parental narcissism on children's lives. The ability to clearly and persuasively articulate the need for legal intervention becomes a determining factor.

e. **Custody Modification Requests and Visitation Restrictions** . In cases of parental narcissism, requests for custody modifications and visitation restrictions may be necessary to safeguard the well-being of the children. Legal intervention focuses on developing solid arguments supported by the evidence presented, seeking to establish agreements that protect minors from the harmful dynamics associated with narcissistic behavior.

f. **Collaboration with Child Protective Services** . In extreme situations, collaboration with child protective services may be necessary. Working together with these services involves sharing relevant information and coordinating actions to guarantee the safety of affected children. Legal intervention becomes a bridge that connects families with the resources necessary to safeguard child well-being.

g. **Continuous Monitoring and Adjustments as Needed** . Once legal measures are implemented, continuous monitoring and adjustments as needed become essential practices. Legal intervention does not conclude with a judicial decision; rather, it requires constant attention to evaluate the effectiveness of the measures implemented and make adjustments as the situation evolves.

h. **Emotional Support for Affected Children and Parents** . Throughout the entire legal process, emotional support for affected children and parents is crucial. Legal intervention is not only about formal measures, but also about providing a compassionate environment that supports the emotional well-being of everyone involved. This support becomes a beacon that illuminates the path towards stability and child protection.

Navigating the waters of legal intervention and child protection in cases of parental narcissism demands a clear strategy, collaboration with competent professionals, and an ongoing commitment to the well-being of children. Legal intervention and child protection act as beacons that guide the path to safety and justice amidst the legal complexities associated with parental narcissism.

8.2. Available Legal Resources: Navigating the Legal Labyrinth in Parental Narcissism Cases

"Available Legal Resources provide practical information on legal tools that can be employed to address risk situations and protect the well-being of the children involved.

- **Restraining and Protective Orders** . Restraining and protective orders are presented as a crucial legal tool in cases of parental narcissism. These orders seek to protect victims from harmful behavior by setting clear limits on the narcissistic parent's interaction. Obtaining such an order can provide an additional layer of security for those affected.

- **Provisional Custody Orders** . In urgent situations, interim custody orders may be requested to ensure the immediate safety of children. These orders allow temporary modification of custody while a more extensive legal process takes place. Its application focuses on protecting minors from possible harm derived from parental narcissism.

- **Psychological Evaluations as Evidence in Legal Cases** . Psychological evaluations are emerging as a critical form of evidence in legal cases involving parental narcissism. Conducted by competent professionals, these evaluations offer a specialized understanding of the impact of narcissistic behavior on family dynamics. The presentation of these evaluations strengthens the legal position by supporting the need for intervention.

- **Supervised Family Mediation** . Supervised family mediation is presented as an option to address conflicts in environments of parental narcissism. Under the supervision of a professional, mediation seeks to find collaborative solutions between the parties involved. This tool can be useful when looking for a more equitable approach, albeit with constant supervision.

- **Parent Coordinators as Communication Facilitators** . In cases where communication between parents is especially difficult, parent coordinators can play a crucial role as communication facilitators. These professionals neutralize tensions and encourage more effective dialogue , seeking to reduce conflicts and promote agreements that benefit children.

- **Lawyers for Children in Legal Procedures** . The participation of children's lawyers in legal proceedings is presented as a way to ensure that the interests and needs of minors are adequately represented. These attorneys focus on advocating for the well-being of children, providing an independent legal voice for their rights and safety.

- **Mandatory Family Therapy Programs** . Some jurisdictions may require participation in mandatory family therapy programs in cases of parental narcissism. These programs seek to address dysfunctional dynamics and provide tools to improve communication and collaboration between parents. Participation in these therapies may be a legal condition for maintaining custody.

- **Support Resources for Victims of Domestic Violence** . In cases where parental narcissism manifests as domestic violence, support resources for victims of domestic violence are essential. These resources include shelters, helplines, and counseling services that offer emotional support and legal guidance to those seeking to escape dangerous situations.

- **Regulation of Digital Contact and Communication** . Within the digital landscape, the regulation of digital contact and communication becomes an important legal resource. Establishing clear guidelines around interaction on digital platforms and electronic communication can help prevent bullying and protect children from narcissistic manipulation through these channels.

- **Legal Resources for Privacy Protection** . Protecting privacy in cases of parental narcissism is vital. Legal remedies for privacy protection seek to safeguard the sensitive information of affected children and parents, preventing its misuse by the narcissistic parent. These resources focus on establishing legal barriers against unauthorized intrusion.

Child protection is a social imperative, and this chapter is presented as a call to action to effectively address the impact of parental narcissism on children's lives and ensure a safer, healthier future.

Chapter 9: The Role of Society and Professionals in Prevention and Treatment

The role of society and professionals in the prevention and treatment of this psychological reality is fundamental. This chapter stands as a call to action, exploring how society and experts can collaborate effectively to prevent and address narcissism in its various manifestations.

9.1. Parental Narcissism Education: Demystifying and Addressing a Contemporary Challenge

Demystifying Parental Narcissism in Society . Education about parental narcissism begins with the demystification of this phenomenon in society.

Disseminating clear and accessible information about what parental narcissism entails, how it manifests itself and what its impacts are, helps dispel myths and misunderstandings surrounding this problem. Clarity in communication becomes the basis for understanding and informed action.

Recognition of Signs and Symptoms by Health Professionals and Educators . To prevent and address parental narcissism, it is crucial for health professionals and educators to recognize the associated signs and symptoms. Specific training on this topic equips these professionals with the ability to identify potentially harmful situations and provide early interventions. Recognition stands as the first line of defense to safeguard the well-being of children.

Integration of Content on Parental Narcissism in Educational Programs . The inclusion of content on parental narcissism in educational programs is presented as an effective strategy to reach a broader audience. Integrating information on this topic into school and vocational training programs helps raise awareness from an early age and prepares future professionals to address situations of parental narcissism with sensitivity and knowledge.

Workshops and Seminars for Parents and Caregivers . Organizing specific workshops and seminars for parents and caregivers becomes an effective platform to provide education on parental narcissism. These events offer a space to discuss family dynamics, share coping strategies, and receive guidance from professionals. Direct interaction becomes a powerful means of transmitting information and fostering dialogue.

Awareness Campaigns in the Media and Social Networks . Awareness campaigns in the media and social networks amplify the reach of education about parental narcissism. Using media platforms to share stories, relevant data and resources can reach diverse audiences. These campaigns seek to not only inform, but also encourage an open conversation about parental narcissism in society.

Development of Accessible Online Educational Resources . The development of accessible online educational resources is presented as a versatile tool to reach a wide audience. Creating digital content, such as videos, infographics, and informative articles, makes it easy to access information about parental narcissism anytime, anywhere. Accessibility becomes a key facilitator for the dissemination of knowledge.

Collaboration with Support Organizations and Professional Associations . Collaboration with support organizations and professional associations strengthens the network of available resources. Working together with entities committed to the prevention and treatment of parental narcissism amplifies the effectiveness of educational initiatives. The synergy between professionals, organizations and society in general becomes a unified front against this challenge.

Promoting Self-Exploration and Help Seeking . Education about parental narcissism seeks not only to inform, but also to promote self-exploration and help-seeking. Encouraging personal reflection on behavioral patterns and offering resources for those seeking support becomes an essential preventive strategy. Promoting early help can make a difference in the lives of those facing this challenge.

Awareness Programs for Legal and Social Services Professionals . To ensure an effective response in cases of parental narcissism, it is crucial to implement awareness programs for legal and social service professionals. These programs provide specific information on how to address legal and social situations related to parental narcissism, enhancing the ability of these professionals to intervene in an informed and sensitive manner.

Continuous Evaluation and Adaptation of Educational Strategies . Education about parental narcissism requires ongoing assessment and adaptation of educational strategies. The evolution of society's understanding and needs demands an agile and flexible response. Constant evaluation ensures that educational strategies are effective and aligned with contemporary challenges associated with parental narcissism.

Education, demystification and informed action are intertwined in the fight against parental narcissism. Education about this contemporary phenomenon not only illuminates the reality of this problem, but also empowers society and professionals to address it with understanding and effectiveness.

9.2. Resources for Mental Health Professionals: Essential Tools in the Prevention and Treatment of Parental Narcissism

<u>**Specialized Training in Addressing Parental Narcissism**</u>

Specialized training is presented as the foundation for mental health professionals in addressing parental narcissism. Specific training programs, workshops and courses offer therapists and psychologists the conceptual and practical tools necessary to understand the complexities of this family dynamic and develop effective intervention strategies.

Clinical Supervision for Cases of Parental Narcissism

Specific clinical supervision for cases of parental narcissism emerges as a valuable tool. The complexity of these family dynamics demands a space for reflection and consultation with experienced clinical supervisors. This practice not only provides guidance, but also contributes to the continued development of specialized clinical skills.

Specific Evaluation and Diagnostic Protocols

Having specific evaluation and diagnosis protocols for parental narcissism is essential. These protocols allow mental health professionals to identify patterns of narcissistic behavior and evaluate the impact on family dynamics. The use of standardized tools improves consistency and precision in case evaluation.

Bibliographic Resources and Specialized Articles

Consulting bibliographic resources and specialized articles acts as a continuous source of knowledge for mental health professionals. Continued research in the academic literature on parental narcissism provides up-to-date information, theoretical perspectives, and innovative strategies that enrich clinical practice.

Collaboration Networks with Other Professionals and Experts

Creating and participating in collaborative networks with other professionals and experts in the field of parental narcissism expands the perspectives and resources available. Establishing connections with colleagues, participating in discussion groups, and attending conferences allow for the sharing of experiences, successful strategies, and challenges, thus strengthening the collective response to parental narcissism.

Specialized Therapeutic Intervention Tools

Access to specialized therapeutic intervention tools is crucial. These tools may include specific therapeutic approaches, tailored intervention techniques, and resources designed to address the particular challenges presented by parental narcissism. Adaptability in therapeutic strategies becomes an essential skill.

Continuing Training in Innovative Therapies

Continuing training in innovative therapies offers mental health professionals an up-to-date perspective on emerging therapeutic approaches. Staying informed about new trends and proven therapies in cases of parental narcissism enriches the clinical repertoire, allowing effective adaptation to the changing needs of patients.

Consultation with Forensic Experts in Legal Cases

In situations involving legal aspects, consultation with forensic experts in cases of parental narcissism is a valuable practice. These experts can provide specialized information that supports clinical work and facilitates the courts' understanding of the complexities of parental narcissism. Collaboration between mental health professionals and forensic experts strengthens the comprehensive response.

Participation in Supervision and Professional Discussion Groups

Participation in professional supervision and discussion groups offers a space to share experiences, challenges and solutions among colleagues. These groups promote an environment of mutual learning and encourage collaboration between mental health professionals dealing with cases of parental narcissism, thus contributing to the continuous improvement of clinical practice.

Access to Emotional Support Resources for Professionals

Access to emotional support resources for mental health professionals is essential in addressing parental narcissism. Given the challenging nature of these cases, having spaces to share the emotional experiences linked to clinical work becomes a key component for the therapist's well-being.

The resources available to mental health professionals intertwine to form a comprehensive set of tools aimed at the prevention and treatment of parental narcissism. Specialized training, clinical supervision, collaborative networks, and therapeutic intervention tools combine to strengthen the capacity of professionals and improve the quality of care in this complex clinical setting.

Chapter 10: Stories of Overcoming and Resilience

In this chapter we will see how testimonies of the human power to face extraordinary challenges, illuminating the path to recovery and transformation after living under the influence of narcissism, will help us work on this topic.

10.1. Testimonials from People Who Have Overcome the Influence of Narcissistic Parents: Voices of Resilience

Filled with resilience, these stories offer us a unique insight into the challenges, struggles, and ultimately triumph over the emotional fallout of narcissistic parenting.

Recognizing the Initial Impact of Narcissistic Influence

The testimonies reveal a common beginning: the recognition of the initial impact of narcissistic influence. Many relate how, in the early stages of their lives, they experienced confusion, low self-esteem, and the feeling of not being enough. The emotional manipulation and lack of empathy on the part of narcissistic parents created complex emotional terrain.

The Process of Awakening and Understanding Family Dynamics

As these people grew up, the process of waking up to and understanding family dynamics became a crucial milestone. Many report moments of clarity, often triggered by external experiences or interaction with supportive figures. This process marked the beginning of the reconstruction of their identity and the understanding that they deserved a life free of the narcissistic shadow.

Coping Strategies Developed Autonomously

Confronting narcissistic influence demanded the adoption of autonomously developed coping strategies. The testimonials reflect a diversity of approaches, from seeking emotional support to setting healthy boundaries. The creativity and determination of these individuals emerge as central elements in their path to recovery.

Establishing Limits and Prioritizing Your Own Well-Being

Limit setting stands out as a common strategy among those who have overcome the influence of narcissistic parents. Learning to say "no," set clear boundaries, and prioritize one's own well-being became a liberating act. These testimonies highlight the importance of emotional autonomy and the ability to make decisions aligned with their own well-being.

Active Search for Professional and Social Support

The active search for professional and social support emerges as a common thread in these stories. Many relate how therapy and connection to supportive communities were essential. These testimonies highlight the importance of having a safe space to express lived experiences and receive guidance from those who understand the complexity of narcissistic influence.

Personal Transformation and Development of Self-Esteem

Personal transformation and the development of self-esteem are vivid testimonies of resilience. Through the active pursuit of self-acceptance and self-love, these individuals were able to free themselves from the emotional chains imposed by narcissistic parenting. Their stories inspire others to embark on a similar journey toward personal reconstruction.

Healthy Relationships and Building Your Own Families

The testimony of those who overcame the influence of narcissistic parents often includes the narrative of building healthy relationships and forming their own families. The ability to learn from past experiences and apply those learnings in new relationships demonstrates resilience and the ability to break harmful family cycles.

Inspiring Others to Face and Overcome Similar Challenges

These testimonies not only share personal experiences, but also serve as a source of inspiration for those facing similar challenges. The resilience of these individuals acts as a guiding light, demonstrating that improvement is possible and that building a fulfilling life after narcissistic parenting is achievable.

Closing Cycles and Personal Empowerment

The closing of cycles becomes a recurring theme in these testimonies. The ability to close painful chapters and move toward personal empowerment manifests as a significant achievement. These individuals, through their stories, convey the idea that the past does not define your future and that resilience can be the cornerstone of a fulfilled life.

Message of Hope for Those Still Struggling

Ultimately, these testimonies convey a message of hope for those still struggling with the influence of narcissistic parents. Resilience and the ability to overcome emotional adversity are presented as a possible path. These stories invite those in the midst of struggle to believe in their own strength and ability to build a healthier, more enriching future.

10.2. Lessons Learned and Practical Advice: Wisdom from Those Who Have Overcome the Influence of

Narcissistic Parents

These voices of resilience not only share their stories, but also offer valuable lessons and guidance for those on the road to recovery.

Cultivate Self-Acceptance and Self-Esteem . A central lesson that stands out is the importance of cultivating self-acceptance and self-esteem. Those who have overcome narcissistic influence emphasize the need to embrace their own self-worth, regardless of the expectations imposed in childhood. Building a positive self-image becomes an essential step towards recovery.

Establish and Maintain Clear Boundaries . The lesson of setting and maintaining clear boundaries is presented as an essential element on the road to recovery. Learning to say "no" and protect yourself emotionally is crucial to avoiding continued manipulation. These individuals advise that firmness in creating boundaries contributes significantly to the preservation of mental health.

Actively Seek Professional and Social Support . The practical advice to actively seek professional and social support resonates in these stories. Therapy, support groups, and connecting with people who understand your experiences become essential elements. Those who have overcome narcissistic influence encourage others not to be afraid to seek help and to build strong support networks.

Learn to Distinguish Between Own and Inherited Responsibility . The lesson of learning to distinguish between one's own and inherited responsibility is crucial. Those who have overcome narcissistic influence share how, by recognizing that they are not responsible for their parents' actions and attitudes, they released significant emotional weight. This discernment allows for greater clarity and autonomy.

Develop Resilience in the Face of Adversity . The ability to develop resilience in the face of adversity is a notable lesson. These individuals emphasize how facing challenges and learning to adapt strengthens emotional resilience. Overcoming obstacles becomes a source of empowerment, demonstrating that adversity can be transformed into an opportunity for personal growth.

Celebrate Small Accomplishments on the Road to Recovery . The practical advice of celebrating small achievements on the road to recovery emerges as a valuable reminder. Those who have overcome narcissistic influence highlight the importance of recognizing and celebrating each progress, no matter how small. These celebrations reinforce self-esteem and motivate us to continue moving forward in the search for a healthier life.

Foster Healthy and Nutritious Relationships . The lesson of fostering healthy, nourishing relationships is a priority. Those who have overcome narcissistic influence advise cultivating positive connections based on mutual respect, empathy and support. These relationships act as a counterweight to toxic family dynamics, providing a space for growth and healing.

Practice Self-Compassion and Patience With Yourself . The importance of practicing self-compassion and patience with oneself is highlighted as an essential lesson. Overcoming the influence of narcissistic parents is a gradual process, and these individuals advise being kind to themselves in times of difficulty. Self-compassion becomes a beacon of light on the journey toward recovery.

Engage the Continuous Self-Discovery Process . The lesson of embracing the process of continuous self-discovery is highlighted by those who have overcome narcissistic influence. Life is a constant journey of learning and growth, and these individuals encourage others to explore new dimensions of themselves, freeing themselves from the limitations imposed in childhood.

Inspire Others By Sharing Your Experiences . Finally, those who have overcome narcissistic influence find meaning in inspiring others by sharing their experiences. Telling stories of improvement is not only therapeutic for them, but also serves as a source of hope and guidance for those who are still in the process of recovery. The act of sharing experiences becomes a gift of resilience for the community.

Chapter 11: Recognizing and Addressing Self-Care on the Journey to Recovery

In this final chapter, we will explore a crucial but often overlooked aspect of the journey to recovery from narcissism in adults: self-care. As we have navigated through the different aspects of narcissism, it is essential to stop and reflect on how individuals can cultivate self-care practices to strengthen their emotional and psychological well-being.

The Central Role of Self-Care in Recovery

Recovery from narcissism not only involves addressing dynamics and patterns in relationships, but also prioritizing personal well-being. This chapter begins with an exploration of why self-care is essential in the recovery process, highlighting its central role in strengthening resilience and building a solid foundation for personal growth.

Identifying and Challenging Limiting Beliefs

Self-care begins with identifying and challenging limiting beliefs ingrained during narcissistic experiences. This chapter addresses how people can work to redefine their perception of themselves, cultivating a healthier and more positive self-image.

Self-Care Practices: A Holistic Approach

From physical care to emotional and spiritual well-being, this chapter explores self-care practices in a holistic sense. Practical and accessible strategies are offered, from incorporating healthy habits to exploring activities that nourish the soul and foster connection with yourself.

Establishing Limits in Self-Care

The ability to set healthy boundaries is essential in self-care during recovery from narcissism. It examines how individuals can learn to say "no," set clear boundaries in relationships, and preserve their emotional energy on the path to healing.

The Role of the Community in Supporting Self-Care

Community and social support are crucial elements in the self-care process. This chapter highlights the importance of building meaningful connections, sharing experiences, and receiving support from those who understand the complexity of recovery from narcissism.

Understanding the Relevance of Self-Care

The path to recovery from narcissism involves, at its core, a deep and sustained transformation. In this context, the importance of self-care lies in its ability to nourish and strengthen the person throughout this process. This section begins with a reflection on why self-care is not just a luxury, but an imperative necessity in the search for mental and emotional health.

Self-Care as an Act of Personal Empowerment

Addressing narcissism requires a courageous act of personal empowerment. Here, we explore how self-care becomes a powerful tool for reclaiming control over one's life and rediscovering authenticity, allowing individuals to move toward a stronger, more conscious version of themselves.

Concrete Self-Care Practices

This section offers a detailed look at specific self-care practices that can be incorporated into your daily routine. From mindfulness and meditation to practicing activities that nurture creativity and personal expression, concrete strategies are presented to cultivate well-being in different dimensions of life.

The Importance of Physical and Emotional Self-Care

Self-care is not limited to emotional aspects; It also encompasses physical well-being. Here, the importance of maintaining healthy habits, from physical activity to a balanced diet, is examined as essential contributions to comprehensive self-care.

Overcoming Obstacles: Self-indulgence as an Act of Self-Love

Self-care is often hindered by patterns ingrained during narcissistic experiences. This section explores how to overcome excessive self-demand and embrace self-indulgence as an act of self-love, allowing yourself to receive the care and attention you deserve.

A Lasting Commitment to Your Own Well-Being. As this additional chapter concludes, the importance of maintaining an enduring commitment to one's own well-being is emphasized. Recovery from narcissism is an ongoing journey, and self-care is presented as an essential tool to cultivate the inner strength necessary to embrace a future full of authenticity, growth, and personal satisfaction.

Conclusion: Toward a Future of Healing and Empowerment

Throughout these pages, we have explored the intricate dynamics that characterize growing up in the shadow of narcissistic parents. On this journey, we have unraveled the emotional and psychological complexities that arise in this environment, but we have also highlighted the possibilities for personal growth and transformation. The conclusion of our journey invites us to look forward, towards a future of healing and empowerment.

At the heart of this journey is unwavering human resilience. Despite the emotional vicissitudes and wounds inflicted by narcissistic parenting, we have witnessed how many individuals have found the strength to face their experiences, understand them, and ultimately seek healing. This resilience is a powerful manifestation of the human capacity to overcome adversity and emerge stronger .

Awareness and deep understanding of narcissistic dynamics are cornerstones on the path to healing. Throughout these pages, we have explored patterns of narcissistic behavior, the impact on children, and strategies for dealing with this challenge. In this process, readers have acquired the tools necessary to identify and understand the narcissistic influence in their lives.

Establishing healthy limits is revealed as an act of self-affirmation and emotional protection. By recognizing the importance of setting clear boundaries in the face of manipulation and lack of empathy, those who have lived under the shadow of narcissistic parents take a crucial step toward emotional autonomy. Likewise, seeking support, whether through therapy, support groups, or meaningful relationships, is presented as a fundamental strategy to not face the challenges derived from narcissistic parenting alone.

The process of closing cycles and healing wounds is an individual journey, but shared by many. The stories of overcoming and resilience, presented throughout these pages, not only inspire, but also point out that healing is possible. By cultivating self-acceptance , establishing healthy relationships, and learning to distinguish between personal and inherited responsibility, individuals have managed to transcend the limitations imposed by narcissistic parenting.

Parental narcissism education not only serves as an identification tool, but also as a means to raise social awareness. Recognizing the influence of narcissism on parenting is the first step in challenging dysfunctional norms and fostering cultural change. This change not only benefits the individuals directly affected, but also contributes to building more understanding and supportive communities.

Legal intervention and child protection emerge as crucial aspects in creating a safe environment for children of narcissistic parents. This chapter not only addresses the legal resources available, but also highlights the collective responsibility of society and professionals to ensure the well-being of the most vulnerable in these family dynamics.

Looking forward involves not only recognizing the wounds of the past, but also projecting a vision for the future based on healing and empowerment. Building healthy relationships, actively seeking emotional support, and cultivating strong self-esteem are essential steps in this journey.

Ultimately, "Narcissistic Parents" not only seeks to provide insight and understanding, but also to act as a beacon of hope. Every word written is intended to offer guidance for those seeking to overcome the after-effects of narcissistic parenting. This book is a testament to the human ability to transform pain into growth, confusion into clarity, and adversity into resilience.

As we close these pages, we carry with us the certainty that the future can be shaped by the choices we make today. May each reader find in these words not only a reflection on the past, but also a map for the journey toward a future of healing and empowerment. Resilience is the compass that guides this path, and the promise of a brighter tomorrow is the star that illuminates the horizon. May healing and empowerment be the keys that open the doors to a future full of possibilities and emotional well-being.

Did you love *Narcissistic Fathers: The Challenge of Being a Son or Daughter of a Narcissistic Father, and How to Overcome It. A Guide to Healing and Recovering After Covert*? Then you should read *Love amidst Anxiety: How to Build Healthy Relationships in Uncertain Times*[1] by Olivia I. Thigpen (ENG)!

2

Discover the path to stronger, more loving relationships amid anxiety and uncertainty!

"Love amidst Anxiety: Building Healthy Relationships in Uncertain Times" is your comprehensive guide to transforming emotional challenges into opportunities for growth and genuine connection.

This book takes you by the hand through the complexities of love in difficult situations. Explore the different types of anxiety that can affect your relationships and learn to recognize the symptoms before they become insurmountable obstacles. Discover the underlying causes of anxiety in the context of relationships and how these worries can strengthen, rather than weaken, your bond.

---

1. https://books2read.com/u/bwQQ2Z

2. https://books2read.com/u/bwQQ2Z

Within these pages, you will find **practical, scientifically supported strategies for managing anxiety both individually and as a couple**. Learn to communicate effectively, even when anxiety threatens to distort your words. Discover how to maintain intimacy and foster deeper connections, even in the most challenging moments.

Additionally, face uncertainty with courage and learn to turn it into an opportunity to strengthen your relationship. This book not only provides you with practical tools to face life's challenges but also provides you with a compassionate and hopeful approach to facing anxiety and uncertainty with your loved one.

"Love amidst Anxiety" is not just a book; **It is an emotional compass that will guide you through storms to more serene and loving waters**. Written with empathy and backed by science, this book will empower you to transform anxiety into an engine of personal growth and lasting love.

Discover how love can flourish even in the darkest moments!

Get your copy now and embark on a transformative journey toward healthy, meaningful relationships.

Also by Alexandria Publications

Extreme Hypnosis for Rapid Weight Loss in Women: Learn How to Lose Weight with Hypnosis and Mental Power.
Learning to Manage Money: Financial Education from Childhood to Adolescence. Teaching Your Children to Save, Spend, and Invest Wisely
Narcissistic Fathers: The Challenge of Being a Son or Daughter of a Narcissistic Father, and How to Overcome It. A Guide to Healing and Recovering After Covert
Narcissistic Mothers: The Truth about Being a Daughter of a Narcissistic Mother, and How to Overcome It. A Guide to Healing and Recovering from Narcissistic Abuse.

About the Author

At Alexandria Publications, we are dedicated to offering quality work supported by experts specialized in various topics. Our commitment to excellence is reflected in every book we publish. We collaborate closely with passionate authors to bring you a wide range of knowledge in various areas. Our mission is to provide you with valuable and enriching readings that feed your curiosity and inspire you to immerse yourself in the fascinating world of knowledge. Welcome to a constant journey of discovery!